1995
B219
Africa

◂ SENEGAL ▸

SENEGAL

William Lutz

CHELSEA HOUSE PUBLISHERS
New York • New Haven • Philadelphia

PP21-005087

Library of Congress Cataloging-in-Publication Data

Lutz, William.
Senegal.
Includes index.

Summary: Surveys the history, topography, economy,
industry, culture, and people of the small country on the
northwest coast of Africa.

1. Senegal. [1. Senegal] I. Title.
DT549.22.L88   1987   966'.3   87-11615

ISBN 1-55546-192-1

1   3   5   7   9   8   6   4   2

Senior Editor: Elizabeth L. Mauro
Editor: Rafaela Ellis
Associate Editor: Melissa Padovani
Copy Editor: Crystal G. Norris
Series Designer: Anita Noble
Designers: Maureen McCafferty, Carol Molyneaux
Production Manager: Brian A. Shulik
Production Assistant: Frances Mullin
Editorial Assistant: Wendy Cox
Series Advisor: Rebecca Stefoff

‹CONTENTS›

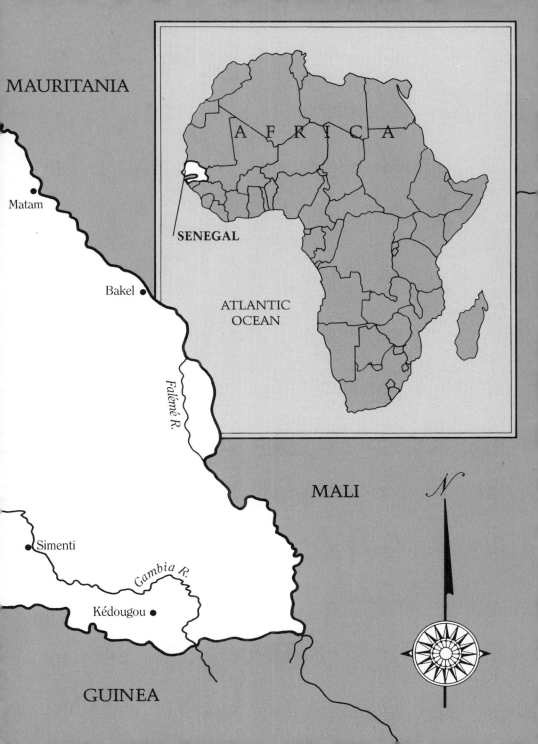

◄ FACTS AT A GLANCE ►

Land and People

Area	75,995 square miles (196,722 square kilometers)
Highest Point	Fouta Djallon Plateau, 1,640 feet (500 meters)
Major Rivers	Senegal, Saloum, Gambia, Casamance
Capital	Dakar (population 1,000,000)
Other Major Cities	Thiès (population 126,886), Kaolack (population 115,679), Saint-Louis (population 96,594)
Population	6,541,000
Population Density	86 people per square mile (33 per sq km)
Population Distribution	Rural, 75 percent; urban, 25 percent
Official Language	French
Literacy Rate	10 percent
Major Ethnic Groups	Wolof, Fulani, Serer, Tukulor, Diola, Malinke, Sarakollé
Religions	Muslim, 90 percent; Christian, 5 percent; animist, 5 percent
Average Life Expectancy	43 years

Economy

Resources	Phosphate, agricultural products
Exports	Petroleum products, peanut oil and peanuts, phosphate, canned and frozen fish

Imports	Crude petroleum, automobiles, sugar, cereals, machinery
Chief Crops	Peanuts (1,000,000 tons, or 900,000 metric tons, per year), cotton, tuna, shrimp
Major Industry	Fertilizer
Employment	Agriculture, 80 percent; mining, manufacturing, and construction, 9 percent; trade, services, government, 7 percent; unemployed, 4 percent
Currency	CFA franc, divided into 100 centimes
Average Annual Income	Equal to $5,160 U.S.

Government

Form of Government	Republic with a 100-member National Assembly and an elected president.
Branches of Government	Legislative, executive, and judicial branches are separate. Members of the legislature and the president serve five-year terms, but the president may serve no more than two terms. The president appoints the Supreme Court.
Head of State	President Abdou Diouf
Subdivisions	Ten regions with governors and capitals

◄HISTORY AT A GLANCE►

by 900 A.D.	Tekrur, on the Senegal River, becomes a flourishing trade center for the Wolof, Fulani, and Serer peoples.
early 1000s	Islam is introduced to Tekrur. Muslim converts soon rule the kingdom under their leader, War Jabi.
1078	The first written account of Senegal appears, written by an Arab traveler who visited the Tekrur kingdom.
1000 to 1400	The Tekrur kingdom grows smaller as some groups break away to form their own kingdoms.
1400s	European explorers move southward along the West African coast in search of a sea route to India. Trading posts are established along the coast.
1445	Portuguese navigators arrive at the mouth of the Senegal River. They also reach the mouth of the Casamance River.
1588	The Dutch take possession of the Portuguese trading post on the small, coastal island of Gorée.
late 1500s	Gorée becomes a major center of the slave trade.
1638	The French build a trading post at the mouth of the Senegal River.
1659	The French settlement is enlarged to form the basis of the future city of Saint-Louis.
about 1680	The French take control of Gorée.
1700s	England and France fight to control trade in West Africa.
1758 to 1763	The British control Gorée.

1809	England again captures Gorée and also Saint-Louis. The British set up a trading post at the mouth of the Gambia River.
1816	The Congress of Vienna restores Gorée and Saint-Louis to France.
1848	The French trading post of Senegal officially becomes a colony.
1854	France appoints Louis Faidherbe governor of the new colony and instructs him to extend French control into the interior.
1855	Faidherbe takes control of the former Wolof state.
1857	The city of Dakar is founded.
1886	The Wolof stage their final revolt against French rule. France now controls all of modern Senegal except the Casamance region.
1879	France allows limited citizenship and self-government for residents of four Senegalese cities.
late 1800s	France uses Senegal as a base from which to extend colonial control throughout much of West Africa.
1902	Dakar becomes the capital of French West Africa (which includes Benin, Niger, Mali, Senegal, Guinea, Ivory Coast, Mauritania, and Upper Volta—one-seventh of the African continent). The city has port facilities and a fast-growing population.
1903	The Casamance region is brought under French control.
1914	Blaise Diagne, the first black African elected to represent Senegal, joins the French Parliament.
1940	France falls to Germany in World War II. The German-controlled Vichy government of France abolishes citizenship and representative assemblies for the Senegalese.
1946	France gives French citizenship to all Senegalese.

1950s	French West Africa experiences a growing movement for independence and self-government.
1958	The Senegalese vote for self-government, with France to remain responsible for foreign relations, defense, higher education, and finance.
1960	Senegal joins the Mali Federation (which also includes French Sudan), then declares independence a few months later. Léopold Sédar Senghor is elected the country's first president.
1981	Senegal and Gambia join their military forces, economic and foreign policies, and communications systems in a limited confederation called Senegambia.
currently	Abdou Diouf, formerly the prime minister, is president.

Although they are poor, the Senegalese enjoy a stable, democratic government.

Senegal
and the World

In today's world, many African countries command front-page newspaper headlines. They attract attention for their conflicts, racial prejudice, disease, famine, and extremist governments. The Republic of Senegal has not been among these newsmakers. Senegal does share some of its African neighbors' problems, particularly the economic ones. Its people are poor—especially by the standards of most well-developed countries. But Senegal's people have not suffered the devastation of those who live in some other African countries, such as Ethiopia. And, although they experience some political problems, Senegalese leaders follow a moderate path. Their actions, therefore, do not attract the kind of attention that extremist leaders such as Libya's Muammar Qaddafi or Uganda's Idi Amin have received.

Senegal may not be in the limelight, but this resilient nation has carved a place for itself in the world. One of Africa's smallest countries, it is located on the western coast. Inland, Senegal borders on Mauritania to the north, Guinea and Guinea-Bissau to the south, and Mali to the east. It also surrounds three sides of the small coastal nation of the Gambia.

Senegal's strategic location has influenced its history and growth. Centuries ago, it was a meeting place for traders from West and North Africa. Later, European explorers prized its natural harbor at the site that today is the capital city, Dakar. It was a stopping point for travelers journeying around Africa to Asia or on their way to South America. And its nearness to shipping routes and to slave dealers in the African interior made it a crossroads for the slave trade. Even today, Senegal is a hub of world trade. It remains a convenient port for ocean traffic bound for Europe and North America.

For much of its recent history, Senegal has had close ties with Europe. At one time a French colony, it grew to become the economic

United Nations workers help Senegalese farmers increase their agricultural output by introducing them to new techniques.

and administrative capital of French West Africa. Although Senegal declared itself independent in 1960, it still retains a strong French flavor. The nation's official language is French, and its school system is modeled on French educational principles. Dakar has a French flair that has earned it the name "the Paris of Africa."

Senegal is also one of Africa's most democratic nations. Unlike many countries on the continent, it has a strong tradition of political freedom. Although many of its neighbors have only one party, Senegal's ballot for a

national election may list candidates from a dozen or more political parties, all of whom campaign openly in speeches and in print.

Many of Senegal's democratic ways were fashioned by Léopold Sédar Senghor, Senegal's first president, who took an independent political stance. He did not align his country with others in international affairs, but he did maintain a close relationship with France. France continues to provide Senegal with much economic aid, and in return, most of Senegal's foreign trade is with France. French military advisers are stationed in Senegal. Senghor's successor, President Abdou Diouf, is also regarded as a moderate and continues many of Senghor's policies.

Although it is independent, Senegal is also very much an African nation. It is a member of the Organization for African Unity (OAU), which was established in 1963. The OAU defends its members' rights to independence and sovereignty and promotes unity and economic development. In July 1985, Senegal's leaders conferred with other OAU members to focus on Africa's economic and agricultural problems. The conference called on each government to increase its farming budget to 25 percent by 1990. It also called for cooperation between African nations and Western creditors to promote economic recovery in the African lands.

Senegal does face problems. Its climate can be oppressively hot, and all too often a devastating drought wrecks a season's planting and forces villagers to relocate in hopes of finding water. Even though the nation has a modern education system, only about 10 percent of its people can read and write. Most Senegalese live in rural villages, yet the majority of health and social workers are based in the cities.

Perhaps Senegal's most serious problem is its economic dependence on one crop: peanuts. Peanuts (also called groundnuts, because they grow underground rather than on trees) form the heart of the country's economy and provide more than half of its export income. Senegal's success in peanut cultivation has made it one of Africa's more economically secure nations. But its economy depends so much on the peanut harvest that a single crop failure can bring economic disaster. To avoid this threat, the government is encouraging farmers to grow a variety of crops and promoting the development of industries that use local resources. Senegalese farmers now grow more crops, some in large enough quantities to export. And industry is expanding, particularly commercial fishing and canneries that package tuna and shrimp for export.

Senegal is attempting to deal with its problems and make the most of its assets, with the help of carefully planned programs. Its domestic programs will improve agricultural production, and its international ones will encourage foreign trade and investment in Senegalese businesses. Senegal's greatest challenge is to improve its economy so that its people can look forward to a brighter future. The Senegalese know their problems cannot be solved quickly, but they persevere. As one of their proverbs advises, "Slowly, slowly—that's how you catch the monkey in the bush."

Senegal's topography varies from region to region. Some areas are infertile and dry, whereas others allow farmers such as this man to grow grains, peanuts, and other crops.

The Land

Senegal is a small country, about the same size as the state of South Dakota. Its location on the western shore of Africa gives it a window on world trade and travel. Because of its location, Senegal is a stopping point on the route around Africa's southern tip, the Cape of Good Hope. It is also a convenient port for ocean traffic bound for Europe and North and South America.

For the most part, Senegal is bordered by water. The Atlantic Ocean forms its western boundary. To the north and northeast, the Senegal River separates the country from Mauritania. And on the east, the Falemé River, a Senegal River tributary, marks the border between Senegal and Mali.

Along with its water boundaries, Senegal has two land borders. One, to the south, separates it from Guinea and Guinea-Bissau. The other border separates Senegal from the Gambia, a country that extends like a finger pointing east for about 200 miles (323 kilometers) into Senegal.

Senegal is a flat country. It covers about 75,995 square miles (196,722 square kilometers) of the large depression known as the Senegal-Mauritanian Basin. Only two areas of the country are more than 330 feet (100 meters) above sea level. One of these areas is the Cape Verde region in the west. It consists of small, hard rock plateaus of volcanic origin. The other area lies to the east and southeast near the border with Guinea. It is part of the Fouta Djallon plateau and represents Senegal's highest point, at 1,640 feet (500 m).

Except for these two areas, most of Senegal consists of plains and gentle foothills, with soil that varies from one area to another. In the northwest, the mustard-colored, iron-rich soil is excellent for cultivating peanuts, the nation's cash crop. In the south, grains and vegetables grow well in clay soil that is also rich in iron. The central area's soil is poorer, supporting sparse grazing for livestock during the rainy season.

Four rivers—the Senegal, the Saloum, the Gambia, and the Casamance—drain Senegal. The Senegal River, which is 1,015 miles (1,633 kilometers) long, is one of the longest rivers in West Africa, stretching from central Guinea through northern Senegal to the Atlantic. When the first explorers from Europe arrived, they traveled this "River of Gold," as they called it, to the area that is now Mali and Guinea. For many years, it was the only means of transportation from the Atlantic coast into the interior. Today, the river remains an important method of transportation.

The size and speed of Senegal's rivers vary considerably from season to season. For example, during the dry season from November to May, the Senegal River flows into the Atlantic Ocean at a rate of about 180 cubic feet per second (5 cubic meters per second). But this flow swells to some 180,000 cubic feet per second (5,000 cubic meters per second) during the rainy season. The river flows through a valley that stretches from Bakel in the east to Dagana in the north. When the rain comes, floods begin in Bakel in early September and reach Dagana by the middle of October. During the rainy season, the river can spread up to 12 miles (20 kilometers) across.

At Dagana, some of the Senegal's waters feed into the Lac du Guiers, a lake 18.6 miles (30 kilometers) long and 3 miles (5 km) wide. This lake provides fresh water for the city of Dakar to the south and yields an annual catch of 2,000 tons (1,800 metric tons) of fish. Also at Dagana, the river spreads out dramatically. This area is called the False Delta. Here, the river's slope is so gentle that, at the height of the dry season, when the river flows most slowly, seawater can back up as far as 125 miles (201 km) inland. For the people downstream who depend on the Senegal for fresh water, this creates a serious water shortage.

As the river reaches the coast of Senegal, it spreads out and floods the land, creating a true delta. However, the Canary Current, a strong ocean current that flows along the coast, forces the mouth of the river southward, creating a long sandspit along the coast called the Langue de Barbarie (Barbary Tongue). The sandspit received its colorful name from sailors who thought it looked like a giant tongue sticking out from what they believed was the Barbary Coast, which is actually farther to the north.

The Climate

Senegal is a tropical country. For most of the year, its climate is hot and dry. In winter, the weather in Senegal is similar to that of the Mediterranean countries. But the weather pattern changes from June to October, when the rainy season arrives, bringing Senegal not only tropical humidity but also swollen rivers and floods.

The seasons rule the lives of Senegalese farmers. From February to May, the heat in the heartland is too oppressive for crop cultivation. Farmers have little work until May or June, when crops are planted in time for the heavy summer rains. Harvest begins in November, and by the following May the last peanuts have been shipped.

Along with Senegal's tropical location, West Africa's prevailing winds also affect the country's weather. These winds fall into two groups: those that are dry, and those that bring rain. The dry winds include trade winds, which blow consistently from one direction. These winds were named by merchant sailors who depended on them to provide predictable routes for their ships. The dry winds also include a dust-laden wind, named the *harmattan* by Arab traders, that blows from the Sahara Desert from November to March each year. The other winds—those that bring rain—arrive in the summer. These are monsoon winds from the west-northwest that swell the rivers and drench the land.

Although all of Senegal experiences dry and rainy seasons, local conditions determine the amount of rainfall each area receives. The northern part of the country lies in the area called the *sahel*—the Arabic word for coast—because it borders on the lower reaches of the Sahara Desert. In

Although crops are planted in time for the summer rains, farmers must sometimes help them along by hand-watering their plots.

this area, the weather is dry and hot, with an average rainfall of only 14 inches (355 millimeters) in the July-to-October rainy season. During this season, temperatures may jump to 95° Fahrenheit (35° Centigrade). The sahel's dry season, which lasts from November to May, is noted for parching dryness and heat. In May, temperatures often soar above 104° F (40° C) and rarely fall below 72° F (22° C). January temperatures are cooler, reaching an average low of 57° F (14° C) shortly before sunrise.

Very different conditions prevail along the 10-mile (16-kilometer) coast from Saint-Louis to Dakar. The winters here are cool, with temperatures falling to lows of about 63° Fahrenheit (17° Centigrade) in January. Even in May, the temperature rarely rises much higher than 81° F (27° C). The rains begin in June, are heaviest in August, and end by October. On average, a year's rainfall totals only about 20 inches (508

Senegalese who work outdoors, like these herdsmen, keep cool in their harsh climate by dressing in loose clothing and covering their heads.

millimeters). This mild weather helps make the coastal area of Senegal popular among tourists.

Most of the rest of the country has a Sudanese climate (like the climate of Sudan, a country in northeastern Africa). It is very hot, humid, and uncomfortable, with heavy rainfall. Around the cities of Kaolack and Tambacounda, in west central Senegal, rainfall averages from 29 to 39 inches (736 to 990 millimeters) each year. Because the rains usually come during the growing season, farmers in this region rarely need to irrigate their fields.

Farther south, in the region around the Gambia River, annual rainfall is even higher, averaging about 50 inches (1,270 millimeters). In this fertile area, vegetation is denser, with light forests and abundant undergrowth.

Still farther south, in the region around the Casamance River, rainfall exceeds 50 inches (1,270 millimeters) each year. The forests in this area are dense, and typical vegetation includes oil palms, mangroves, and rice.

Plant and Animal Life

Regional differences in climate and in soil content account for Senegal's wide variety of vegetation. Almost 25 percent of the country is suitable for growing crops, from peanuts and sorghum grasses to corn, beans, sweet potatoes, and rice. Another 30 percent of the country is suitable for grazing animals. The savannas—grassy plains with scattered trees and drought-resistant undergrowth—are ideal for raising livestock, including cattle, goats, sheep, pigs, horses, camels, and donkeys. Savanna grass grows sparsely in the northern part of the country and the central Ferlo Desert region and more thickly in the southern region.

Forests cover about 28 percent of Senegal. Much of the forestland is in the lush Casamance region, but these forests yield few commercial products. Elsewhere in the country, acacia trees are a source of gum arabic, a resin used in making a variety of products from adhesives to candy.

Along the Atlantic coast, from the city of Saint-Louis south to the Gambia border, palms, ironwoods, and citrus trees flourish. Vegetables grow well here, too. But many of the large animals that once populated this area have been driven inland by the growing population.

Animals of the African plains and jungles still survive in Senegal's interior. Elephants, lions, antelopes, panthers, cheetahs, and jackals live as they have for centuries, although in far fewer numbers. In the marsh country, particularly in the False Delta, warthogs are common. Along the Senegal River's banks, warthogs, hedgehogs, and monitor lizards live, along with such fish-eating, wading birds as spoonbills, egrets, and other herons.

The forests along the Gambia and Casamance rivers are filled with many types of monkeys. Southern forests are home to pythons and boa constrictors, as well as to cobras and a variety of other poisonous snakes. The rivers are also populated with water-dwelling mammals and reptiles, including crocodiles, hippopotamuses, and turtles. Smaller wild animals are more common. Hares, for example, thrive throughout Senegal. Partridges and guinea fowl also can be found in many parts of the country. Unfortunately for grain farmers, so can large numbers of tiny birds called *quelea*, or millet-eaters. These birds can eat a farmer's entire crop.

Most Senegalese belong to one of three ethnic groups that have occupied the area since the 11th century. Now united into one nation, these tribes once lived separately.

The Road to Independence

Senegal has no written history of its very early years, so little is known about the country's first inhabitants. Some experts believe that these people migrated west from the Nile River valley, but little evidence exists to support this theory.

Senegal's earliest written history comes from an Arab named El Bekri. In 1078, he described the kingdom of Tekrur, located along the Senegal River at Fouta Toro. Its peoples, he said, included Wolofs, Serers, and Fulani—three of the major Senegalese ethnic groups that exist today—and its boundaries stretched from the Senegal River to the edge of the Sahara Desert.

Tekrur's advantageous location had already made the kingdom a flourishing trade center by the time El Bekri wrote about it. West African merchants brought slaves, gold, and kola nuts north to Tekrur. There they traded their goods for weapons, glossy seashells called cowries—used as money in many parts of West Africa—and salt from rock-salt deposits in the Sahara.

By the same time, the Islamic religion, which had been introduced to the area by North African traders and Muslim missionaries, had begun to take hold. Early in the 11th century, the Zenaga Berbers of Mauritania had established a Muslim monastery on an island in the lower Senegal

River. Soon afterward, a chief named War Jabi converted to Islam. He and his new Muslim converts took control of the kingdom of Tekrur—from which they took their name, Tukulor—and formed an alliance with neighboring Berber Arabs, the Almoravids.

During the next 400 years, the kingdom of Tekrur grew gradually smaller and weaker as people of different ethnic groups broke away from Tukulor rule and carved out their own kingdoms. The Wolof kingdom, for example, was established when its peoples broke away in the 15th century and claimed the land between Cape Verde and the Senegal River. But, like Tekrur and other African kingdoms, the Wolof kingdom came under increasing pressures. Before the end of the 18th century, five major states had struggled free of Wolof rule. Each of these tribal states ruled its people independently until the French conquered them all in the late 19th century.

For many years, then, each Senegalese ethnic group governed itself. This long history of independent tribal rule may be one reason that Senegal has remained free of the intergroup rivalries that have caused mistrust and sometimes even warfare in many other African countries.

Precolonial History

During the 15th century, European explorers first began to move south along the African coast, hoping to find a sea route around Africa to India. Although the dangers of exploration were great, so were the potential rewards: fabulous riches from gold, silk, and especially spices.

Portuguese seamen, searching for good harbors to set up profitable trading posts, slowly worked their way down the coast of West Africa. At first they found only the harsh, uninhabited coast of Morocco and the western Sahara. But they continued to push south because the ocean along the coast provided rich fishing grounds, and because they met Arabs who were willing to trade gold for Portuguese goods.

In 1445, Portuguese navigators arrived at the mouth of the Senegal River. They continued south along the coast to the mouth of the Casamance River. Africans today jokingly call these Portuguese explorers the first tourists to visit Africa—but their arrival marked a turning point in the histories of Senegal and the continent.

Along the coast, the Portuguese newcomers established trading posts that slowly changed West African trade. Little by little, merchants shifted their trade routes from the desert to the coast. Many of the great cities that had grown up along the desert trade route declined, and some disappeared forever, while the coastal towns grew quickly. The Portuguese set up posts on Gorée, a small island just 2 miles (3.2 kilometers) off the coast of Senegal, and at Ziguinchor on the Casamance River. Here they traded for hides, gum arabic, gold, and slaves. Gorée in particular became a major port for slave ships for the next three centuries.

Before long, other European nations wanted to participate in the rich trade with West Africa. The Dutch took possession of Gorée from the Portuguese in 1588 but eventually lost the island to the French. Meanwhile, the French explored the Senegal River as far as Fouta, and the British investigated the Gambia River. In 1638, a Frenchman built a trading post at the mouth of the Senegal River. In 1659, Louis Caullier expanded that French settlement by establishing what would become the city of Saint-Louis on the island of N'Dar.

During the next 40 years, control of West African trade seesawed back and forth between the French and the British. In 1809, the British captured the city of Saint-Louis and the island of Gorée. Seven years later, the peace treaty that ended the Napoleonic Wars between France and England returned Saint-Louis and Gorée to the French. Meanwhile, the British had established outposts at the mouth of the Gambia River. On the Falemé River, the French built trading posts and forts and purchased the islands of Diogue and Carabane from native kings.

In 1848, the French coastal trading posts officially became a colony of France. Six years later, Louis Faidherbe was appointed governor and given a free hand to extend French control up the Senegal River. Faidherbe, a 36-year-old army engineer, scholar, and linguist, set out to

France appointed Faidherbe governor of its trading posts in the Senegal region.

establish a base from which the French could defend their commerce and take control of African land trade routes. His plan involved enlarging the colony through conquest of the interior.

Faidherbe first defeated the Moors of Trarza, who had a thriving gum trade on both sides of the Senegal River. In 1855, he took control of the former Wolof state of Walo and built forts at Matam, Bakel, and other sites along the Senegal River. His aim was to halt the westward advance of warring Muslim rulers, especially the religious leader Al Haj Umar Tall. Faidherbe successfully defended the French territory against Tall's *jihad*, or holy war. Tall was forced to turn eastward to continue his Islamic reform movement. Later in the 19th century, other Muslim rulers made Islam a rallying point for Senegalese resistance to the French. The resistance they roused was often widespread. But by 1886, after the last unsuccessful Wolof opposition effort, the French were in firm control of all of Senegal except the Casamance region.

Twenty years after Tall's turnaround, France used Senegal as a base for its campaign to control the rest of West and North Africa. Sweeping eastward from the Atlantic Ocean to the Nile River, the French force conquered all the land before it. In Senegal, by 1903, even the Casamance region had submitted to French rule. The colonial era had begun.

Colonization

French West Africa consisted of a federation of eight territories: Benin, Guinea, Mali, the Ivory Coast, Mauritania, Niger, Senegal, and Upper Volta (now called Burkina Faso). It covered an area of about 1,789,000 square miles (4,634,000 square kilometers), amounting to roughly one-seventh of the total land area of the African continent. In 1902, Dakar, a city founded in 1857, became the capital of French West Africa. France ruled over its West African lands from 1895 until 1958.

To make Dakar the showcase of French West Africa's economy, the French pumped money into the city. Soon Dakar became the federation's principal port. Its modern conveniences appealed to French and other European trading companies that established overseas headquarters there. Before long, Dakar became larger than Saint-Louis. About 10 percent of its inhabitants were French, making Dakar the largest European community in West Africa.

As Dakar grew and flourished, so did Senegal's economy—thanks to peanut exports. Cultivation of the peanut crop was encouraged by French administrators, starting with Louis Faidherbe. As a result, peanut exports steadily boosted Senegal's status as the wealthiest colony in French West Africa.

Meanwhile, the country was going through political growing pains. The French government began a policy of "assimilation," trying to mold the people of Senegal according to French ways. In 1879, the French government introduced an elected General Council and established municipal councils based on the French example. French law gave French citizenship to Senegalese born in the four urban areas of Dakar, Gorée, Rufisque, and Saint-Louis. This meant they were ruled by the same laws as residents of French *communes* (townships) and entitled to the same rights, including the right to local self-government, the right to vote, and the right to hold elective office. These rights were restricted to men only, as they

The island of Gorée became one of four French communes whose residents were entitled to French citizenship and other rights.

were in France at the time. And in Senegal, they applied only to those in the communes. Rural Senegalese were not citizens but "subjects," with far fewer rights—a difference that eventually led to tension between these two groups.

Citizens also had the right to elect a representative to the Chamber of Deputies, which was the French parliament in Paris. The first black African to hold this post was Blaise Diagne, a colonial customs official who

served from 1914 to 1934. During World War I (from 1914 to 1918), Diagne helped enlist large numbers of Senegalese in the French army. He undertook this effort in return for a French guarantee of permanent citizenship for black Africans in the four communes, at a time when some politicians, both in France and in Africa, were considering ending that status.

In the 20 years between the two World Wars (from 1919 to 1939), Senegal faced economic difficulties. As the resources devoted to peanut production grew, production of other food crops diminished. Peanut farming costs went up in relation to the price paid for the crop. And most of the profit went to foreign companies and colonial banks, not to the farmers.

With World War II came a major political setback. France fell to the Nazis in 1940, and the government installed by Adolf Hitler did away with Senegal's representative assemblies and stripped the Senegalese of their French citizenship. It also drained the country's resources to support the Nazi war effort.

After the war, Senegal's colonial status changed again. In 1946, the French government, having been released from Nazi domination, recognized all Senegalese as French citizens. For the second time, the colony became an overseas territory of France. The French government maintained strict control of Senegal. Although French officials tried to introduce reforms, they were unable to improve rural living standards.

In Senegal, as in other nations of French West Africa, cries for independence grew louder through the early and middle 1950s. Among those who appealed to French President Charles de Gaulle was Léopold Sédar Senghor, one of Senegal's two representatives to the French Chamber of Deputies. In 1958, de Gaulle responded by offering the French West African nations three choices: complete independence, continued colonial status, or self-government within the French community. Under the third alternative, France would continue to be responsible for foreign relations, finance, defense, and higher education. Senegalese voters, like those in all the other territories except Guinea (which chose independence), chose the

After Senegal gained independence, Senghor (left) met with French president de Gaulle.

third alternative. Senghor and many other leaders saw this choice as an intermediate step toward eventual independence.

The final steps toward Senegalese independence came in 1960. That April, France recognized Senegal as part of the Mali Federation, which also included French Sudan. By August 20, 1960, Senegal had left the federation and established itself as an independent nation.

Today, the beautiful island of Gorée is a major tourist center. But for three centuries, it was an island of horror where thousands were sold into slavery.

Island of Slaves

Just a 2-mile (3-kilometer) ferry ride from Dakar lies the island of Gorée. Although it is small—only about 88 acres (36 hectares) in area—and largely barren of vegetation, the island attracts many visitors. Its sandy beaches, washed by deep-blue Atlantic waters, are perfect for sunbathing, swimming, and picnicking. Cars are banned, so tourists can stroll through the narrow island streets and shop for souvenirs and for local arts and crafts. The spicy aromas of cooking, both Senegalese and French, and the sounds of lively bargaining fill the air. The orange tile roofs of island houses glitter in the sun. And one of Senegal's most beautiful hotels, the Relais de l'Espadon—once the mansion of the French governor-general—overlooks it all.

Today, Gorée is a major tourist center, a historical reserve with attractive inns, museums, and shops. But it was not always so pleasant. For 300 years, Gorée was the shipping center for much of West Africa's slave trade.

Gorée's connection with the slave trade and other trade began after Portuguese navigators arrived there in the 15th century. The nearly barren, rocky island offered a protected position against attack from the Senegalese mainland, so the cautious Europeans established a base there. Gorée quickly became an important relay point for Portuguese ships making the long journey from Lisbon to ports in Brazil and the West Indies.

Because the island's location gave it control of the natural harbor on the mainland that today is the port of Dakar, control of Gorée meant control of the gateway to West Africa.

That control became increasingly desirable as trade between Europe and West Africa grew. Gold and ivory were the earliest attractions, but African traders could also supply European buyers with exotic animal skins, tanned leather, amber, musk, and slaves. France, England, Portugal, and the Netherlands each were eager to have all of the profits of this rich trade, not merely a share. So along with waging war to subdue the inhabitants of West Africa, these European countries waged war against each other to win Gorée.

As a result, control of Gorée shifted repeatedly. In 1588, the Dutch wrested Gorée from the Portuguese. On November 1, 1677, a French fleet took Gorée from the Dutch, and the French moved quickly to make the island a military stronghold and the center of their trade. They also made treaties with local kings to guarantee themselves a monopoly on trade along the Senegalese coast.

In 1692, the British conquered Gorée, but the French regained control within a few months. From 1758 to 1763, the British again took possession; then the French returned. The British won the island again in 1809 and kept it until 1816, when the Congress of Vienna restored it to the French. From that time until Senegal became independent, France controlled Gorée.

While control of Gorée shifted, one fact remained constant: the island was a major collection and shipping point for the transatlantic slave market. For perhaps hundreds of thousands of enslaved men, women, and children, Gorée was the last stop before leaving Africa.

Traders brought slaves to Gorée from villages in the African interior and locked them inside "slave castles," buildings used as temporary housing. There the slaves awaited the ships that would transport them to the slave markets and plantations of North or South America. During the three or four months they might spend there, they were packed tightly into windowless rooms. Anyone who rebelled was chained to the wall. Slaves who tried to escape were thrown from the cliffs into the shark-infested ocean. As a result of the miserable living conditions and the harsh treatment, many of the slaves died on the island. More died on the ocean voyage—as many as half of the people taken from their African homes did not survive the transatlantic trip.

But slavery and the slave trade had existed in Africa long before the first Portuguese sailor ever set foot on Gorée. In Senegal, for example, perhaps more than half of the population belonged to one of several slave classes.

An African could become a slave in several different ways. He could be born into a slave family. If he were a criminal, his chief could sell him as punishment. He could sell himself or be sold by his family to obtain food during a famine. A gang of slavers might kidnap him. Or, if he were a prisoner of war, his captors could make him a slave.

Unless a slave had been a prisoner of war or a criminal, his life probably was not all that different from a free African's. He might have a piece of land to farm for himself, and he might be free to marry and raise a family as he wished. A member of the warrior-slave class could achieve high standing in society, become wealthy, and even own slaves himself.

Slave life became much harder after the African slave trade became big business. When Europeans began colonizing the new lands that had been claimed by explorers such as Christopher Columbus, Ferdinand Magellan, and Vasco da Gama, slaves were in big demand to work the sugar, cotton, and coffee plantations in the New World. Africans who could withstand hard work in hot climates became a dependable source of labor for the people who bought and used them.

Although the English, Dutch, Portuguese, French, and other Europeans became actively involved in the slave trade, fear of tropical diseases kept most of them from traveling into the African interior and capturing slaves themselves. Instead, they established outposts on the coast where they bought or traded for slaves from African chiefs and kings. This coop-

As European profits mounted, countless Senegalese fell victim to the cruel trade.

erative system between Europeans and Africans enabled both buyers and sellers to make much money quickly. The profit motive kept the slave trade alive for more than 300 years.

But in the late 18th century, a popular movement to abolish slavery arose in Europe and America. It was fueled by political and religious reform. England declared slavery illegal in 1807. Other countries followed suit. When France abolished slavery in 1848, Gorée's slave-exporting days ended.

Although the slave trade died, the French continued to extend their control over West Africa. Gorée's importance declined because its port could not handle the growing shipping demands of government and commerce. Dakar's importance increased as a result. As Dakar's harbor grew, Senegal's economic center shifted to the mainland, and Gorée ceased to be of much value.

Today, little remains of the dark days of slavery on Gorée. The major remnant is the Maison des Esclaves, or House of Slaves. This slave castle, built in about 1776—the year that independence was proclaimed in the United States—is preserved as it was when slaves were jammed into holding rooms in its basement. The only difference is that present-day Senegalese have inscribed freedom slogans on the walls where slaves were once chained.

In only about an hour, a visitor can walk Gorée's narrow streets, which wind past whitewashed old houses, small inns, and restaurants. The battlements of the 19th-century fort at the southern tip of the island offer a magnificent view of the ocean, the bay, and the shore of Senegal.

On the northern tip of the island is the Fort d'Estrées, or the North Battery, which today serves as a prison. The oldest building on Gorée is the police office. Built in 1482, it was originally a Portuguese church. Then it became, in turn, a warehouse, forge, bakery, guardhouse, fish market, and dispensary. In another slave house, built between 1777 and 1807, the Basic Research Institute of Black Africa has opened a museum. St. Charles Borromeo Catholic Church, built between 1825 and 1829, is located not far from one of Senegal's oldest mosques. Everywhere the island is full of a sense of history, as well as the remains of all of the cultures that have washed over and influenced both Gorée and Senegal.

A love of family and children unites all of Senegal's people, regardless of their tribal affiliation. Other similarities include the Wolof language, which most Senegalese speak.

The People–
Variety and Unity

Today, Senegal has a population of 6,541,000. The population growth rate is high, increasing by almost 3 percent each year. About 40 percent of all Senegalese are younger than age 15.

Senegal's population includes members of seven major ethnic groups and a few smaller ones. The largest group is the Wolof (sometimes spelled Ouolof), which makes up about 36 percent of the population. Other major groups are the Fulani, the Serer, the Tukulor, the Diola, the Malinke, and the Sarakollé. Although every ethnic group has its own language, most Senegalese can communicate in the Wolof language. Some social scientists believe a process they call "Wolofization" is taking place, in which smaller groups are becoming more like the Wolof majority as more and more Senegalese leave their home villages for school or work in the cities.

The Wolof are the most influential as well as the largest ethnic group in Senegal. Wolof farmers are the primary growers of peanuts. They also produce millet (a grain whose seeds can be ground into flour) and sorghum (another grain that can also be ground or used as fodder for cattle).

Not all Wolof are farmers, however. Many have left their farms for Dakar and other cities. Working as merchants, goldsmiths, tailors, carpenters, teachers, and civil servants, they have achieved prominence among the educated people of Senegal.

Like many other ethnic groups in West Africa, the Wolof tribe once had a very rigid society. A chief was at its head, and its people were divided into clearly defined castes or social classes. Traditionally, these castes included royalty, an aristocracy, a warrior class, common people, artisans, and slaves. Everyone was born into one of these castes and could never move into another. Today, however, this caste system has virtually disappeared.

The Wolof are Muslims, and most belong to one of two fairly strict Islamic sects, the Tijani or the Mourides. Islam permits polygamy (marriage to more than one spouse), and the laws of Senegal allow Muslim men to have two wives—within certain limits. When a man first marries, he must state in an official document whether he plans to take a second wife. He does not have to take a second wife if he makes this declaration, but he may not take a second wife if he doesn't. The typical Wolof family consists of a husband, a wife or wives, and children. Other relatives may also live with the family.

The Fulani, the second largest ethnic group in Senegal, are also known as the Peul, Fulbe, Foulah, and Fellata. Originally a nomadic people, they can be found today throughout West Africa but especially in Senegal, Mali, Nigeria, Guinea, Cameroon, and Niger. Most Senegalese Fulani live in the Ferlo and Upper Casamance regions.

As nomadic herdsmen, the Fulani traditionally followed their livestock to wherever they could find grazing land. In their wanderings, they came in contact with a number of different cultures and absorbed parts of many of them. Over the years, therefore, their own culture and ethnic makeup have changed a great deal.

Today some Fulani have settled as farmers while others still lead nomadic lives. The farmers live in villages and are strict Muslims. But nomadic Fulani still wander in groups, making temporary camps and living in portable huts. They are less strict in observing Islamic practices, and some still practice the traditional African religion of animism—a belief that plants, animals, rocks, and water, as well as human beings, contain a

(continued on page 57)

SCENES OF
SENEGAL

◄ *In the cities, people in traditional garb mix with those in Western-style dress.*

◄ *In an effort to diversify the farm economy, Senegalese farmers are planting more rice.*

➤ *A Senegalese mother often carries her baby on her back.*

➤ *Using a small combine, two farm workers strip grains of rice from their stalks.*

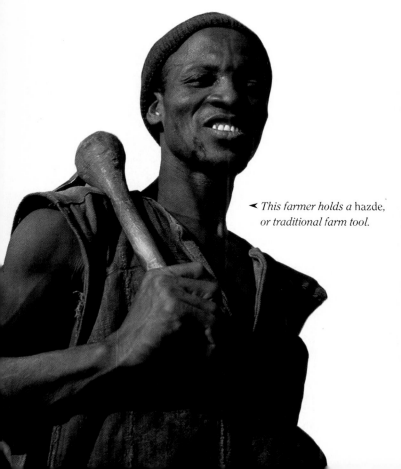

◄ *This farmer holds a hazde, or traditional farm tool.*

⋏ *Senegalese men prepare to launch a brightly colored boat into the Atlantic Ocean.*

⋎ *A planting program has reforested this hillside with lush evergreen trees.*

➤ *Dressed in a Western suit jacket, this rice farmer prepares for a day's planting.*

⌄ *Farmers watch a demonstration.*

∧ *Senegalese women work as hard in the fields as in the home. These women harvest rice.*

➤ *Peanuts, called groundnuts by the Senegalese, are the nation's most important crop.*

➤ *Dakar's port is the center of the import and export trade.*

∨ *Using a long-toothed tool, these farmers prepare a field for planting rice shoots.*

(continued from page 48)

nyama (spiritual force) that unifies everything. So real is this belief that children may run away from a camera for fear that a photograph will diminish their nyama.

Like the Wolof, the Fulani practice polygamy. But unlike the Wolof, the Fulani have never had a rigid social order. All members of the tribe are treated equally and have equal status.

The Serer are Senegal's third largest ethnic group. Many of them live in the western part of the southern Ferlo region, which is the country's most fertile peanut-growing area. They are productive farmers, who grow not only large amounts of peanuts but other crops as well. They also raise cattle. Originally animists, more and more Serer are converting to Islam or Catholicism. Léopold Sédar Senghor, Senegal's first president, is a Catholic Serer. His successor, Abdou Diouf, is a Muslim Serer.

The Tukulor (or Toucouleur), who take their name from the ancient kingdom of Tekrur, make up Senegal's fourth largest ethnic group. But because they have intermarried with the Wolof and Fulani for many years, they are difficult to distinguish as a separate ethnic group today. Over the centuries, this mingling of the groups has left the Tukulor little of their distinctive, traditional culture.

Today, many Tukulor live as farmers in the middle part of the Senegal River valley, the Fouta region in the southeast, and between Bakel and Dagana. Some Tukulor can also be found living along the Gambia and Saloum rivers. Many have abandoned farming and moved to Dakar and Saint-Louis.

Under their 11th-century leader War Jabi, the Tukulor were the first Senegalese people to convert to Islam. Even today, many of the Tukulor are literate in Arabic because that is the language of the Koran, Islam's holy book. They have the reputation of being the most devout of Senegal's ethnic groups.

The Diola, members of another ethnic group of about the same size as the Tukulor, live mostly in the lower Casamance River valley and the southwestern part of the Gambia River valley. Expert farmers, they are particularly adept at growing rice, a crop upon which much of Senegal depends for food. But to avoid this risky dependence on a single crop, the Diola have begun to diversify in recent years by raising peanuts and millet.

Traditionally, the Diola have kept apart from the mainstream of Senegalese society. Their religious practices are typical of their independent ways: most Diola are animists, although some are Muslim or Christian.

The Malinke (also called the Mandinka or Mandingo) came originally from the Niger River valley. Today they live in many parts of Senegal, especially in the Gambia, Saloum, and upper Casamance river valleys.

Besides being expert farmers who grow a variety of crops, the Malinke conduct a vigorous trade in food and other products along the rivers on

In recent years, many farm people have packed their donkeys and moved to the city.

which they live. Happy with their lifestyles, few Malinke have moved to the cities. They are fervent Muslims—although, like many other groups, they retain some elements of animism. They practice polygamy.

The Sarakollé (or Soninke), the smallest of the major ethnic groups, live in Senegal and in neighboring Mali. They are descended from the Berbers, Arab tribesmen who roamed the North African deserts and raided West Africa. By tradition they are farmers, but years of drought have made their land unproductive. Many have abandoned their farms and moved to the cities, where they are small-scale traders and merchants. Although many of them are Muslims, they have not lost their animist beliefs.

The ornate Grand Mosque is a holy shrine for the millions of Senegalese who practice Islam.

Perhaps the best-known of Senegal's minor ethnic groups is the Lebu, who live in the Cape Verde region. They were the first Africans the Portuguese encountered on Senegal's coast more than 500 years ago. Now, as then, the Lebu are fishermen, living on the coast and tending their boats and nets. Many are also wealthy landowners.

Of the non-Africans who live in Senegal, the two largest groups—of about 15,000 people each—are the French and the Lebanese. Both groups reside almost entirely in the cities. The French population has decreased as the number of Senegalese with enough education for executive and managerial jobs in industry and government has grown. But the number of Lebanese—who first arrived during the colonial era—has stabilized. Today many of them operate shops and small restaurants.

About 80 percent of the Senegalese people speak the Wolof language, yet the country's official language is still French. Like most African nations, Senegal for centuries had no written language. Instead, information was preserved verbally—passed down from generation to generation by the spoken word.

Although some modern Senegalese authors have written their works in Wolof, the language has no formal grammar or spelling rules. Even its alphabet is uncertain. Writers have used both Latin and Arabic characters, but some educators are pushing for a Wolof alphabet. Many Senegalese believe that the use of Wolof as a written and a spoken language, with a grammar and vocabulary to be studied, will not only promote literacy but also will help bring the different ethnic groups closer together.

Here are some Wolof words and phrases:

Na nga def?	How are you?
Maa ngi fi rekk.	I am fine.
Jere-jef.	Thank you.
Bi, naata la?	How much is this?
Waaw.	Yes.
Deedeet.	No.

Every Senegalese village has a market where local artisans can sell their hand-crafted pottery and other wares.

In the Villages and Cities

Most Senegalese—about 80 percent of the country's 6.5 million people—work in agriculture. So it is not surprising that only about 20 percent of the population lives in urban areas. The rest lives in villages.

Most of Senegal's 13,000 villages are quite small, with no more than 200 people. The reason for their limited size is a practical one: the villagers must walk to the fields they cultivate. Keeping the village small lets all the inhabitants live within easy walking distance of their work.

Most villages share some basic features: a public gathering place with plenty of shade from the hot midday sun; a mosque (Muslim place of worship); and a well, spring, or other source of water. The head administrator of the village is the chief, who is either appointed by the government or nominated by the villagers. Muslim villages also have a *marabout*, a wise man who can read and write Arabic and who is well-versed in the Koran. He directs the village's religious life and in many cases is influential in its political life as well. Beyond these common features, local conditions and ethnic traditions influence the size, structure, and organization of each Senegalese village.

Like the bull's-eye of a target, a Wolof village is located at the center of three ring-shaped areas. Each ring is reserved for growing certain kinds of crops. The outermost ring, farthest from the village, is called the *gor*. It contains fields for such cereal crops as millet and sorghum. The middle ring is called the *diatte*. It usually contains peanut fields. The innermost ring is called the *tol-keur*, which means "kitchen garden." It contains vegetable gardens and other small plots.

The women and children in the village usually tend the fields in the first circle; the men tend the farther fields in the second and third circles. During the busy harvest time, all of the villagers work in all of the fields.

After the harvest, villagers store their crops in granaries made of woven straw, located far from the houses as a precaution against fire. If a spark from a cooking fire were to set the granary on fire, a village could lose its entire food supply, and its people could face starvation.

The Wolof build their small houses of locally available materials, such as mud or clay brick. Many houses have roofs of corrugated metal. In some parts of Senegal, Wolof villagers build houses that can easily be moved from place to place. That way, if the water supply dries up, or if the ground proves bad for crops, the villagers can pack up their homes and belongings and settle in another place.

Quite different from Wolof villages are the Malinke villages in the Sudanic region of the Casamance River valley. In a typical Malinke village, 200 to 300 people live in a walled compound of rectangular huts that are crowded together and aligned in geometrical order. This arrangement dates back to precolonial times, when it protected a region under constant attack by invaders from the north.

In addition to farming, the Malinke raise livestock, such as goats. The animals' grazing fields are usually farther from the village than the cultivated land, which needs closer attention.

The Serer are culturally related to the Wolof, but their villages are like no others in Senegal. Each village is a collection of compounds. The compounds may be widely scattered, and each compound, called a *m'bind*, contains the houses of all members of a single family. The houses are trim, neat, and solidly built, usually of brick. A granary in each compound holds the grain and other crops the family harvests from the surrounding fields.

Each compound is an independent unit, responsible for running its own affairs. The Serer village is organized around the family, and the family is little affected by outside authority, whether civil or religious. This means that a Serer chief has considerably less power and prestige than the chief of a Wolof or Malinke village. Although many of the Serer have become Muslims in recent years, many others are Catholics, so most villages do not have marabouts.

Diola villages are the largest and most developed villages in Senegal. Some contain as many as 5,000 inhabitants. Most Diola are rice farmers, and they traditionally locate their villages close to their fields—usually on an overlooking plateau or ridge.

Within the Diola village, the arrangement of houses follows no particular order. The houses themselves are among the best built and most permanent in Senegal. In fact, their construction is so sturdy that some villages look almost like fortresses. Some villages have community facilities to meet particular needs—systems to collect rainwater and store it in a central water tank, for example.

Like a Serer chief, a Diola chief has only limited authority and has little of the prestige of Wolof or Malinke chiefs. Because most of the Diola continue to practice their traditional animist religion, their villages do not have marabouts.

For most Senegalese who have moved to the cities, ethnic distinctions have dissolved as improved salaries, jobs, and education have created a new social class. In Dakar, for example, modern city apartments and suburban houses are home to a middle and upper-middle class of government officials, business executives, and professionals whose lives are not much different from those of Europeans in similar positions. But the cities still have a significant population of unskilled and semiskilled laborers whose lives are similar to the hard lives of agricultural workers in the villages. One of the greatest challenges facing Senegal's leaders is to broaden economic opportunities to give all of the country's people, both urban and rural, a future with greater security.

Most villages have a community well where villagers can draw water.

Senegalese Cities

With five major population centers—Dakar, Saint-Louis, Thiès, Kaolack, and Ziguinchor—Senegal is one of the most urban countries in Africa. Most of these centers started as colonial outposts, and many still retain some colonial flavor in their architecture and layout.

Dakar, the capital, is one of Africa's largest cities, but it is important for more than its size. Its cultural, political, and economic prominence have made it the unofficial capital of West Africa. Its European style and appearance have earned it the nickname "the Paris of Africa."

Dakar's name comes from a Senegalese word for the tamarind tree, a locally grown tree with tough, yellow wood and red-striped yellow flowers. Tradition holds that early navigators asked the name of the settlement that is Dakar today by pointing toward the little cluster of houses they saw on the shore. The villagers, who thought the foreigners were pointing to the trees, answered *"n'dakar"*—"tamarind tree."

In some ways, Dakar was destined to be an important city from the beginning. It offered the largest natural harbor on Africa's west coast, a harbor that beckoned to European explorers in search of sea routes around Africa to India and the Orient. In addition, Dakar's strategic location at the tip of West Africa gave it convenient access to a thriving European sea trade.

But it wasn't until 1857 that the French formally established the city. At that time, sea trade was increasing. The small, rocky island of Gorée could not serve the ever-growing number of ships coming to Senegal. So the French turned to Dakar.

Dakar grew rapidly. In 1866, the French built a pier on Dakar Point to accommodate ships sailing to South America, some 1,620 miles (2,613 kilometers) to the west. In 1885, the government opened West Africa's first railroad, connecting Dakar and Saint-Louis. The railroad stimulated economic development—especially the peanut crop—all along its route. Soon Dakar was the shipping point for peanuts and other goods brought to it by rail.

As Dakar's economic importance grew, so did its political importance. In 1902, it became the capital of the eight-nation Federation of French West Africa. When Senegal gained independence in 1960, Dakar remained its capital.

Today, Dakar has a population of about 1 million people and is an interesting mix of traditional African culture and present-day customs. It is a modern city of tall buildings, wide boulevards, and rush-hour traffic jams. Yet it reflects its African heritage. On a busy main street, a visitor may see two businessmen with expensive leather briefcases walking together, one in a tailored suit and the other in traditional African robes. Likewise, it is not uncommon to see one Senegalese woman in the latest Paris fashion a few feet from another woman in a brilliantly colored, starched *boubou* (long dress) and head scarf.

Like most large cities, Dakar is divided into districts. The southern district contains public buildings, hospitals, embassies, and the Pasteur Institute (a world-famous center of medical research). The business district in the north centers on Independence Square and is surrounded by markets, light industry, and sports stadiums for soccer and wrestling matches. Farther north and east is the port of Dakar, with its naval arsenal, fishing harbor, and export facilities.

Although 75 percent of Senegalese live in rural villages, the nation's cities are quite modern. Dakar rivals a Western city.

For the shopper, Dakar offers three main markets. Kermel market is famous for its flowers. But it also has merchants selling fruits and vegetables, gold and silver jewelry, wood carvings, metal sculptures, woven baskets of all shapes and sizes, and many other items. Sandaga market is more like a giant supermarket, specializing in food, including spices, candy, and condiments. Some Sandaga merchants also offer kitchen utensils, hardware, and small furnishings. Still others sell the brilliantly colored cloth used in traditional Senegalese clothing—and can make it up into a shirt or boubou while the customer waits.

Tilene market is located in the "Medina," the low-income "people's town." It is where most of Dakar's Senegalese inhabitants do their daily food shopping. Here, too, tailors sell cloth and sew garments, silversmiths and goldsmiths work at their benches, cooks fry exotic dishes, merchants sell fresh fish—and all are packed into a space so small it is a wonder they can even move.

Just 164 miles (264 kilometers) north of Dakar is Saint-Louis. This is Senegal's oldest city, established by the French in 1659. Located on an island at the mouth of the Senegal River, it is connected to the mainland by the Pont Faidherbe (Faidherbe Bridge), which is named after the first colonial governor.

Many of the old buildings in the northern half of Saint-Louis recall the city's colonial background. The governor's palace, built as a fort in the 18th century, today serves as a government building. An old, residential section where the French merchants, civil servants, and military officers lived is clustered around Place Faidherbe, a long, rectangular public square in the heart of the city. The houses in this section, painted in hues of blue, rose, orange, and yellow, are set off by balconies and verandas built to take advantage of cooling sea breezes.

Saint-Louis's southern half, called Guet N'Dar, is much different from the northern section. It is home to the fishermen of Saint-Louis, whose square huts with conical roofs are clustered throughout the area. At the doors of the huts are stands at which the fishermen, in wool caps and oilskin coats, hawk the catch of the day to the bustling shoppers.

Forty-five miles (70 kilometers) inland from Dakar lies Thiès. The city was founded in 1862 by Governor Faidherbe to provide a communications point between Dakar and Saint-Louis, and it grew in importance after the 1885 completion of the railway linking those cities. Today, this city of more than 100,000 is Senegal's transportation hub. Virtually all roads—and railroads—lead to Thiès.

<71>

Country farmers sell their wares at city markets, such as this one in Saint-Louis.

Like Dakar, Thiès is laid out like a French city—with wide, spacious avenues, sidewalk cafés, numerous public squares, and tree-lined streets. But mixed with the flavor of 19th-century France is that of a modern African industrial city. This unique combination gives Thiès a character unlike that of any other city in Senegal. An industrial center, Thiès contains an aluminum-manufacturing plant, farm equipment manufacturers, cotton-spinning and cloth-weaving factories, cement plants, a tannery, railroad-equipment repair shops, phosphate processors, and peanut processors.

Employment opportunities in these factories have lured large numbers of workers to Thiès from rural areas, making the city a melting pot of ethnic and religious groups. Shops and street vendors line its streets, offering fruit, cakes, peanuts, fans, handkerchiefs, and dozens of other items.

Thiès is also the home of two government-sponsored centers for local handiwork: the Senegalese Manufacturers of Decorative Arts, for tapestry weavers, and the African Cultural Center, where other artists and craftsmen make and sell work in wood, metal, and other materials.

Outside of Thiès grow some of the most spectacular stands of baobab trees in Senegal. With their stark, spiky, almost leafless branches, these massive trees stretch across the landscape.

Kaolack, located 114 miles (183 kilometers) southeast of Dakar, has a population of about 150,000. The "peanut capital" of Senegal, the city is the shipping center for the 600,000 tons of peanuts produced each year in the surrounding Sine Saloum region. East of Kaolack, peanut plantations stretch as far as the eye can see, and mountains of peanuts, still on the stalk, are piled in the sun to dry. A large portion of each crop is processed into salted peanuts.

Peanuts are not the only crop produced around Kaolack. A smaller volume of cashew trees is grown here as well—not only for nuts, but also for cashew fruit, which looks something like an apple and can be eaten or used to make a kind of brandy. The Senegalese government plans to plant thousands more cashew trees to increase revenue from this valuable crop. Other crops grown around Kaolack include melons, tomatoes, cabbage, lettuce, eggplant, and carrots.

Near Kaolack are some of the most interesting archaeological sites in Senegal. Southwest of the city, along the Bao Bolong River, are ancient megaliths (huge blocks of carved stone) arranged in three large circles: one with 10 stones, one with 11, and one with 14. On the other side of the river, in the village of Diallo Kouma, is another circle of these stones with a burial ground in its center.

Ziguinchor, on the Casamance River, has a long history. The Portuguese made it the capital of their colony of Guinea in the 16th century. In 1854, it became a French settlement. Today it is the capital of the Casamance region and an important economic center. Three large bridges now link the city to the river shores, boosting its chances for growth.

In tiny, seaside villages, the waterfront becomes a marketplace where farmers sell produce.

Other towns of interest include Cap Skirring, a tiny village on the extreme southern limit of the Casamance River that is now home to a major resort complex. Called an "earthly paradise" by the Senegalese, it is rapidly becoming an internationally famous tourist site.

Touba is Senegal's holy place: the birthplace of Mouridism, one of the country's major Islamic sects. Because of its religious significance, tens of thousands of pilgrims visit Touba each year. They come from Senegal and elsewhere in Muslim Africa to visit its mosque and to pray.

The Richard-Toll Dam, built by Senegal in cooperation with the governments of Mali and Mauritania, has provided the base for an agricultural business complex employing 8,000 people. Water from the dam irrigates a major sugarcane plantation. A refinery has been built nearby to process the cane into sugar and other products. The government is also developing wheat and corn production in the area.

Pottery, woodcarving, and weaving are among the many crafts practiced by Senegalese artisans. The Artisan Training Centre in Dakar preserves traditional arts.

A Culture of
Many Flavors

Throughout Senegal, art, sculpture, music, and dance influence people's lives. At times, particularly in sophisticated Dakar or Saint-Louis, the arts retain a European flavor carried over from the days of French rule. But the roots of Senegal's culture sprouted many centuries before the arrival of the first French administrators, Portuguese explorers, and Arab travelers.

An important cultural element that is just as active today as in Senegal's ancient past is the *griot*, a figure unlike any in European or American culture. The griot was and continues to be many things: a musician, a poet, a historian, a paid publicity agent. In some ways, he is similar to the wandering medieval minstrel, traveling from town to town with his collection of songs and stories.

But the griot is more than that. He is also a man of learning and common sense, paid to tell the truth and to relate it with great wit. The griot knows almost everything about his region, public and private. He fulfills the role of village newspaper, town memory, and public record. He may recite poems, tales of great warriors, or the history of a village. In a country with no written language, the griot was the preserver of history, literature, and song. Even today—when he may accompany his songs on a traditional instrument like the *cora* or an electric guitar—he is as important to the culture of Senegal as he ever was.

Just as the written word has had little to do with the preservation of Senegal's history, so the written note has been of little importance in the country's music. Instead, both traditional and pop-style musicians build their works around improvisation and strong rhythms, frequently composing songs that are irresistible for dancing and quite pointed in their comments on current events.

A basic part of the Senegalese rhythms is the drum. In Senegal, no celebration begins without a drum. Drums come in shapes, sizes, and

In addition to preserving Senegal's heritage, training programs such as this weaving class teach young people marketable skills.

forms that are as different as one village is from another. Some are tall, others short. Some have single drum heads, some double. Some rest on the ground, others on the drummers' collar bones.

Drums are just one of many traditional Senegalese instruments. The *balafon* is a sort of xylophone that produces a soft, rippling sound when its wooden keys tap gourds of different sizes. Other instruments, particularly stringed ones, are also made from gourds. The wide variety of gourd shapes and sizes permits almost countless variations, from the lutelike

cora, with its 21 strings, to the 4-, 5-, and 9-stringed *hoddou riti* and the single-stringed *khalam*. Wind instruments include 2- and 3-hole flutes made from millet stalks and trumpets fashioned from antelope horns.

Like music, dance is a vital form of expression in Senegalese life. No event, public or private, in village or city, is complete without dancing. The national dance troupe, which is based in Dakar, performs internationally as well as at home.

Another part of Senegal's rich cultural tradition is the variety of work produced by the country's artisans, craftspeople, and other artists. To demonstrate this work, the government opened the seaside Soumbedioune Artisan Village outside Dakar in 1961. It is a place for artists and craftspeople to make and sell their works. The objects produced there range from wood carvings and pottery to traditional clothing, gold and silver work, delicately formed metal statuettes, baskets in every shape and size, and jewelry of all colors and designs.

Thiès is the site of the Senegalese Manufacturers of Decorative Arts, noted for woven cloth and tapestries. These weavings, renowned for their original, distinctive design and superb craftsmanship, may command prices of more than $1,000 per square foot (9.2 square decimeters). The Art Institute in Dakar also displays and sells tapestries and paintings by the country's most noted artists.

In addition to music, dance, and other decorative arts, Senegal has a strong tradition of sculpture. Usually abstract in form, most sculptures suggest the artists' ideas and feelings about the subjects rather than faithfully reproducing them. A sculpture of a gazelle, for example, may convey the animal's grace and rhythm through an abstract image of only the horns and neck.

Although Senegal is only now developing its own written language, many Senegalese have published works in French. Among the most notable of the country's authors is Léopold Sédar Senghor, the first president of the republic. A scholar, philosopher, and poet of international reputation, Senghor has enthusiastically encouraged the development of literature and the arts in Senegal. In 1984, he achieved France's highest intellectual honor, becoming the first African ever elected to the Académie Française.

Other notable Senegalese writers include former National Assembly President Mamadou Cisse Dia, a playwright and historian. Novelist and movie director Ousmane Sembene has won international recognition for his films. Birago Diop's collection of folktales and sayings, the *Tales of Ahmadou-Koumba*, has helped spread the country's traditional literature beyond the range of the griots. These and other writers are helping Senegal develop a written literature to match the richness of its oral tradition.

Besides providing cultural food for the mind, Senegal has its own methods for preparing food for the body. Senegalese cooking, very much like the Creole cooking found in New Orleans, may be one of Africa's most flavorful food traditions. Peppers and other spices, added generously to rice, vegetable, seafood, and chicken dishes, give Senegalese food a distinctive sharpness. The national specialty is a stew made of rice, fish, oysters, shrimp, and other seafood. It is called *tieboudien* in Wolof. In the side streets and the market districts of Dakar, inexpensive little restaurants called "tieb shops" serve big bowls of the filling stew for the equivalent of a dollar or two.

Senegal has become a leader in African politics. In 1986, President Diouf represented African nations in a speech before the United Nations.

Government and Economy

Although Senegal's political system today generally works smoothly, the nation's path to independence from France had some rocky spots. The traditions of almost 150 years, during which Senegal was first a French protectorate, then a colony, and finally an overseas territory, bound the two nations together politically, economically, and culturally. The nationalist leaders who saw the need for Senegal's eventual separation from France were divided between those who wanted a complete break and those who saw advantages in maintaining friendly relations with the mother country.

In 1956, France's Parliament gave Senegal and the other French West African territories a large degree of self-government. A number of African leaders, however, saw that the establishment of territorial governments would likely result in the creation of many small states and work against the development of national unity. Fearing this outcome, they opposed this change in government policy.

Among the leaders opposing France's decision was Senegal's Léopold Sédar Senghor. Before World War II, he had been a highly respected teacher in Tours, France. Drafted into French military service, he was captured by Nazi troops in 1940. He survived two years in prisoner-of-war camps, there writing some of his most notable poems, before escaping and becoming part of the French Underground (a resistance movement against the Nazis). After the war, he took part in the Constituent Assembly that France held to determine its future relationship with its colonies, and he became one of Senegal's two deputies to the French National Assembly. He was the first African to hold a seat in the French cabinet. In 1956, he was elected mayor of Thiès and reelected deputy.

By 1959, Senghor's efforts to foster African unity led to an alliance of Senegal, French Sudan, Dahomey, and Upper Volta in a union known as the Mali Federation. At the same time, he appealed to France's President Charles de Gaulle to grant Senegal independence.

In April 1960, France and the United Nations recognized the Mali Federation as an independent state. But when Senegal and French Sudan

A body of 100 deputies comprises the National Assembly, Senegal's legislature. The assembly meets in this building in Dakar.

found it impossible to merge their interests, the federation disintegrated. On August 20, 1960, Senegal declared itself a separate republic. A month later, French Sudan did likewise, changing its name to Mali.

In 1960, while still a member of the Mali Federation, Senegal adopted its first constitution, which called for a parliamentary system of government. Then, after the federation dissolved, Senegal adopted a dual executive system of government, with a president and prime minister.

Senghor, who had earned a reputation as a distinguished poet, politician, and statesman, became the Republic of Senegal's first president. He and Prime Minister Mamadou Dia governed together until December 1962, when Dia attempted to seize power in a coup d'etat (overthrow of the government). President Senghor and the Senegalese Army overcame Dia's effort without bloodshed. A court tried Dia and sentenced him to life imprisonment, but President Senghor released him in 1974. (Soon afterward, Dia resumed a leading role in one of Senegal's major political parties.)

In 1963, after the failed coup, Senegal adopted a new constitution. The constitution has been amended several times since then, most recently in 1983. As presently written, it separates executive, legislative, and judicial powers and features a strong, centralized presidential regime. The office of prime minister has been abolished, and the president governs directly. He appoints all ministers, but he does not have the power to dissolve the National Assembly, the country's legislative body.

Senegal's constitution proclaims a commitment to fundamental human rights and a respect for political, trade-union, and religious freedom. The Senegalese state, according to its constitution, is a social democratic state. It recognizes no state religion. The president is elected by the people and can serve no more than two five-year terms. The National Assembly is made up of 100 deputies who also are elected every five years. The president appoints the Supreme Court. Until 1981, the constitution limited the number of political parties in the country to four. An amendment that year removed the limit, and the number jumped to 15 by 1984.

For administrative purposes, Senegal is divided into ten regions, each with its own governor and capital. Each region is divided into three provinces, and each province is further divided into several districts, or *arrondissements*.

As a leading nation in West Africa, Senegal takes an active interest in the affairs of its neighbors. When, in 1981, rebels in the Gambia staged a coup, Senegal responded to a request from the government and sent troops to restore order. In November of that year, Senegal and the Gambia agreed to merge as a limited confederation called Senegambia. The pact called for the two nations to combine their military and security forces, form an economic and monetary union, and coordinate their foreign policies and communications facilities.

On January 1, 1981, Léopold Sédar Senghor retired, to be replaced by the man he had groomed as his successor, Prime Minister Abdou Diouf. In April 1983, Diouf was reelected, winning 80 percent of the popular vote. A few months later, the National Assembly amended the constitution to eliminate the position of prime minister.

Education

Fewer than 10 percent of Senegal's people are able to read and write. The government realizes that, to improve the country's standard of living, it must improve its literacy rate. Thus, education has become a high priority. School attendance is compulsory for children between ages 6 and 14. The dropout rate is high, however, and overall attendance figures are low. In 1984, for example, only 53 percent of school-age children attended school. Attendance is lower in rural areas than in towns, and lower for girls than for boys. Even in more densely populated areas, where school attendance is highest, less than 40 percent of school-age girls attend school.

The major reason for such poor attendance is economic: not many families can afford to have their children in school. In rural areas, children are needed to help in the fields. In the cities, many children must find a job or become part of a family business as soon as they are old enough to

The government attempts to increase the literacy rate by encouraging school attendance.

work. A secondary but still powerful reason for poor school attendance is the language barrier. Almost all schools teach in French, Senegal's official language, but most Senegalese children do not speak French.

The French connection to education is deeply rooted in Senegal's past. When Senegal was the administrative center of French West Africa, French colonial officials brought in French educators who built a school system that would prepare students to become government employees and leaders. The Senegalese school system still follows the French model.

The French founded two of the oldest and most prominent secondary schools (*lycées* in French) in Africa: the Lycée Faidherbe in Saint-Louis and the Lycée Van Vollenhoven in Dakar. More recently, Senegal has built a number of technical schools, including two in Dakar and one in Saint-Louis, where the course of study is more practical and job-related than in the academically oriented lycées.

For students who pursue their educations beyond the lycée, the University of Dakar has become one of Africa's best centers of learning. Today, it has close to 12,000 students. More than half of them come from other countries to study in Dakar. Established in 1957, the university offers degrees in law, economics, medicine, pharmacy, science, humanities, veterinary science, computer science, and library science. Until 1968, when the university refocused much of its curriculum on African studies, a degree in any subject from the University of Dakar was equivalent to the same degree from a French university. For degrees in medicine, this is still true.

Despite the problem of low school attendance, the demand for higher education in Senegal has become so great that the nation is building a second university at Saint-Louis. Some Senegalese have sought higher education outside their country. About 4,000 Senegalese students are enrolled at universities abroad—many in France, other European countries, and North America.

Transportation

Just as its educational system is rooted in its French heritage, Senegal's rail and road systems were also first established by the French. Most of the railways and roads are concentrated in the western part of the country, serving major urban centers.

Senegal has 6,000 miles (9,600 kilometers) of roads, but only about 25 percent of them are paved. The railroad system consists of two main lines that meet at Thiès. One line runs from Saint-Louis to Dakar, and the other goes from Dakar to Koulikoro on the Niger River. Both lines have branches into the country's interior.

Dakar's airport, Dakar-Yoff, serves international as well as domestic travelers. The Concorde, the French supersonic airliner, makes regular flights there. Air Afrique, a multinational airline in which Senegal has a share, flies regularly from Dakar to New York and Paris, as well as to several African countries. The airline also provides domestic service to local airports at Thiès, Saint-Louis, Ziguinchor, Kaolack, Rosso, Podor, Matam, Tambacounda, Kedougou, Sementi, and Kolda. An agreement signed between Senegal and the United States may bring yet another kind of aircraft to Senegal in the future: the American space shuttle may some-day use Dakar-Yoff as a landing base.

Senegal has seaport facilities at four cities—Dakar, Kaolack, Ziguin-chor, and Saint-Louis—but only Dakar can handle large international ships. Although Dakar is the port for Senegal's imports and exports, its overall traffic has fallen off somewhat since 1960, when the countries of French West Africa became independent nations and started to compete for business. Dakar's chief competition for passenger and shipping traffic today comes from two ports, Nouadibou in Mauritania and Las Palmas in the Canary Islands.

River transportation was crucial to Senegal's early development. It became less important as the railroads and paved roads reached into the country's interior. But in a few remote areas, river traffic goes on even today.

One problem with river transport is its seasonal nature. On the Sene-gal River, small cargo vessels can navigate inland about 175 miles (292 kilometers), from Saint-Louis to Podor, all year long. But only from early August to early October, when rain swells the river, can cargo move to other cities farther inland, such as Kayes in Mali.

Neither of the country's other two main rivers, the Saloum and the Casamance, is a major shipping artery. Still, brightly painted, shallow-draft canoes called *pirogues,* which can travel where bigger boats cannot, carry a great deal of local cargo and passengers from place to place on both rivers. On the Saloum River, traffic centers on Kaolack, Senegal's main peanut port. On the Casamance River, most traffic passes through the port of Ziguinchor.

Economy

Senegal's economy is mainly agricultural. About 80 percent of working people are involved in farming. And the farmers' single most important product, which forms the keystone of the country's economy, is peanuts.

Because the port at Dakar can handle huge freighters, it is Senegal's major trade port.

Peanut sales to France, other European countries, neighboring African countries, Japan, and other nations provide about 80 percent of Senegal's earnings from exported goods. In an average year, nearly 3 million acres (1,200,000 hectares) of farmland produce about 1 million tons (.9 million metric tons) of peanuts. "When peanuts do well," the Senegalese say, "we all do well."

But when peanuts do not do well, Senegal's economy plunges. In 1970, for example, production fell, and the country teetered on the edge of economic disaster. For that reason, the government is encouraging farmers to grow a variety of crops and it is seeking to develop industries that make use of local resources. Senegalese farmers now grow enough cotton so that some can be exported. Commercial fishing is an expanding industry, and Senegalese canneries package tuna and shrimp for export.

Decreasing its economic dependence on a single crop is not the only reason Senegal needs to widen its agricultural focus. The country has not been able to produce enough food to feed its people. The 630,000 tons (547,000 metric tons) of grain the country produces in a good year satisfy only about half of its food needs. In a poor year, grain output may meet only one-quarter of the country's need. To reduce Senegal's reliance on expensive imports such as sugar and rice, the government is encouraging farmers to grow significant quantities of rice, millet, corn, beans, sweet potatoes, and cassava (a starchy plant from whose roots flour is made). And plans call for irrigation projects, particularly in areas where rice grows well, to make more land available for cultivation.

Along with growing a greater abundance and wider variety of agricultural products, Senegal needs to strengthen other parts of its economy. Although it is more industrialized than any of the other former federation countries, it has few factories and produces few manufactured goods. The only item Senegal produces in large quantities for export is commercial fertilizer, made from the phosphates that are its most abundant mineral. The country makes only enough of its other manufactured goods to satisfy the domestic market.

International groups work to help Senegal improve its economy. A Peace Corps volunteer (center) helps women dig a compost heap.

Senegal needs to expand and strengthen its economy because of the changes brought by independence. Before French West Africa broke up, Senegal was its economic center. Senegalese industrial plants processed much of the federation's exports, and Senegalese ports were vital for shipping. Now, however, the newly independent countries in the federation are less dependent on Senegal.

To boost the Senegalese economy, the government has several projects underway. One agreement with Mali and Mauritania involves construction of the Richard-Toll dam and its surrounding farming and manufacturing facilities. The same three-way agreement provides for a second dam, in Mali, that will benefit citizens of all three countries.

Even as it moves forward, Senegal clings to its past. A street scene mixes cars and cattle.

Looking Ahead

The small, strategically located country of Senegal has long been one of Africa's busiest, most cosmopolitan lands. Its rich past has contributed much toward its present status as a peaceful, stable nation working to make the most of its attributes.

One of Senegal's earliest civilizations, the Tekrur kingdom, flourished in the 11th century A.D. In the 1500s, Portuguese traders established posts on Senegal's coast. A succession of other European merchants followed, eager to benefit from the gold and slaves brought to Senegal by Arab and African traders.

France eventually gained control of a large portion of West Africa, including the Senegal region. The French developed the colony's cities, as well as its systems of government, economy, and education. Senegal became independent in 1960. Under its first president, Léopold Sédar Senghor, it adopted a constitution establishing its present form of government.

Today, the government of President Abdou Diouf is working to improve Senegal's economy and the standard of living of its people. Like many African nations, Senegal faces a combination of problems and undeveloped potential. Its basic structures—government, education, and transportation—are better developed than those of its neighbors. Yet still

Rural health clinics provide services to villagers who would otherwise lack medical care.

it must cope with many of the problems that its neighbors face. Among the most pressing problems are a high population growth rate and the periodic, unpredictable threat of drought. The nation also faces the problem of offering too few jobs—especially higher-level jobs for the young people graduating from its schools. Because the economy is concentrated in urban areas, the vast rural population can find no jobs other than farming. In addition, social and medical services are inadequate in the countryside. Perhaps Senegal's greatest challenge is to improve economic opportunities so its people can look to a better, more secure future.

Senegal recognizes its challenges and is working to meet them. The government has begun a major effort to establish clinics for basic health care and health education in outlying areas. Projects such as the Richard-Toll energy and agricultural complex are making inroads against unemployment. New and different kinds of crops are reducing the country's dependence on its peanut harvest and increasing its ability to feed its people. The government's agricultural agents visit the villages, bringing tools and modern methods to increase the farmers' efficiency and productivity. Iron ore has been discovered in eastern Senegal, and the government has encouraged international investment in a multinational concern to develop new industry there.

Even the perpetual and unpredictable enemy, drought, is being tamed. Senegal sponsored an international conference to examine the problem of desertification—the gradual expansion of desert areas into the sahel. As desert areas expand, less land remains for cultivation. The government has plans to fight back with reforestation and irrigation projects. And it is encouraging other African countries to join in these efforts.

Senegal's solid government and institutions are not the only reason that the country may be in a better position to move forward than many of its neighbors. Another reason is its people. Despite the diversity of its ethnic and religious groups, Senegal is a country whose people are united—proud of their heritage as Serer or Fulani or Malinke or Wolof, as Muslim or Christian or animist, but also proud of their identity as Senegalese. The spirit of cooperation this unity creates will serve them well as they work to build a country in which they and their children can enjoy a better future.

‹G L O S S A R Y›

Animism   The philosophy, held by many Africans, that all natural things—people, plants, animals, and stones—possess souls, through which the gods watch and influence everyday human life.

Assimilation   A French policy of the late 19th century, aimed at teaching the Senegalese the French language and making them part of the French community.

Balafon   A xylophone-like instrument made of hollow gourds that are struck by wooden keys.

Boubou   A woman's long dress, usually made of brightly colored cloth.

Commune   One of four urban areas in which the Senegalese were granted French citizenship and some political rights between 1879 and World War II.

Cora   The traditional instrument of the Senegalese griot. It resembles a lute or guitar with 21 strings.

Desertification   The gradual encroachment of the Sahara Desert southward into the sahel, drying out farm and pastureland and thereby making them useless.

Diatte   The middle of the three agricultural rings surrounding a Wolof village, where peanuts are usually cultivated.

Gor   The outermost ring of cultivation around a Wolof village, where cereal crops are grown.

Griot   An important figure in Senegalese cultural life, the griot is a wandering musician-poet-storyteller. He preserves and passes on the history and legends of a people with little or no written literature.

Groundnuts	Another name for peanuts, given because they grow underground. They are used throughout Africa.
Gum arabic	The resin of the acacia tree, used in making candy, medicines, and adhesives. Gum arabic received its name because it was sought by Arab traders who entered West Africa many centuries ago.
Harmattan	The Arab word for the hot, dry wind that begins in the Sahara Desert and blows across Africa. It sweeps over Senegal from November to March.
Hoddou riti	A lute or guitar with four, five, or nine strings.
Jihad	An Islamic holy war—that is, any war between Muslims and non-Muslims.
Khalam	A one-stringed lute or guitar.
Mali Federation	A short-lived federation made up of French Sudan and Senegal. They joined together in 1960 but soon declared individual independence.
Marabout	A Muslim holy man who can read and write Arabic and is familiar with the Koran, the Islamic holy book. He interprets holy scriptures and laws for his village and often has some political power in addition to his religious importance.
M'bind	A compound or walled cluster of houses in a Serer village. All of the houses in a m'bind are occupied by members of the same family.
Mosque	The Muslim house of worship, often topped by a dome and decorated with tiles in geometric patterns.
Nyama	The spirit force believed by animists to live in all natural things.
Organization of African Unity (OAU)	An international organization founded to improve trade between African nations and to better the standard of living of their people.
Polygamy	The practice of marriage by one man to more than one woman. Polygamy is practiced in many African countries and in Islamic cultures all over the world.

Sahel The Arabic word for "coast." Also the northern region of Senegal that borders on the Sahara Desert.

Savanna A tropical or subtropical grassland containing scattered trees and drought-resistant undergrowth. Savannas are usually home to herds of grazing animals.

Slave castles Former temporary housing on the island of Gorée for slaves who were shipped to Europe or the New World. Only one remains standing today.

Tol-keur The innermost of the three agricultural rings around a Wolof village. Used for growing vegetables.

Wolofization The process whereby smaller tribal groups within Senegal are gradually blending into the Wolof majority by adopting the Wolof language and customs.

◄INDEX►

ACKNOWLEDGMENTS

The author and publisher are grateful to the following sources for photographs: AP/Wide World Photo (pp. 39, 80); Professor A. Ford/Imagefinders (pp. 36–37, 40, 68–69, 92, 94); Library of Congress (pp. 14, 26–27, 30, 34, 44, 46, 50–51, 53, 58–59, 66, 73); The Peace Corps (pp. 60, 82–83, 86, 91); Margaret Rulon-Miller/Stock Market Photo Agency (pp. 49, 51); The United Nations (pp. 2, 16–17, 62, 71, 74, 76–77); World Bank (pp. 20, 24–25, 50, 52a, 52b, 52–53, 54a, 54b, 55a, 55b, 56a, 56b, 89). Photo research: Maggie Berkvist; Imagefinders, Inc.